THE TREE-MENDOUS RAINFOREST!

ALL ABOUT THE RAINFORESTS
CHILDREN'S NATURE BOOKS

Speedy Publishing LLC

40 E. Main St. #1156

Newark, DE 19711

www.speedypublishing.com

Copyright 2017

All Rights reserved. No part of this book may be reproduced or used in any way or form or by any means whether electronic or mechanical, this means that you cannot record or photocopy any material ideas or tips that are provided in this book.

In this book, we're going to talk about rainforests around the world. So, let's get right to it!

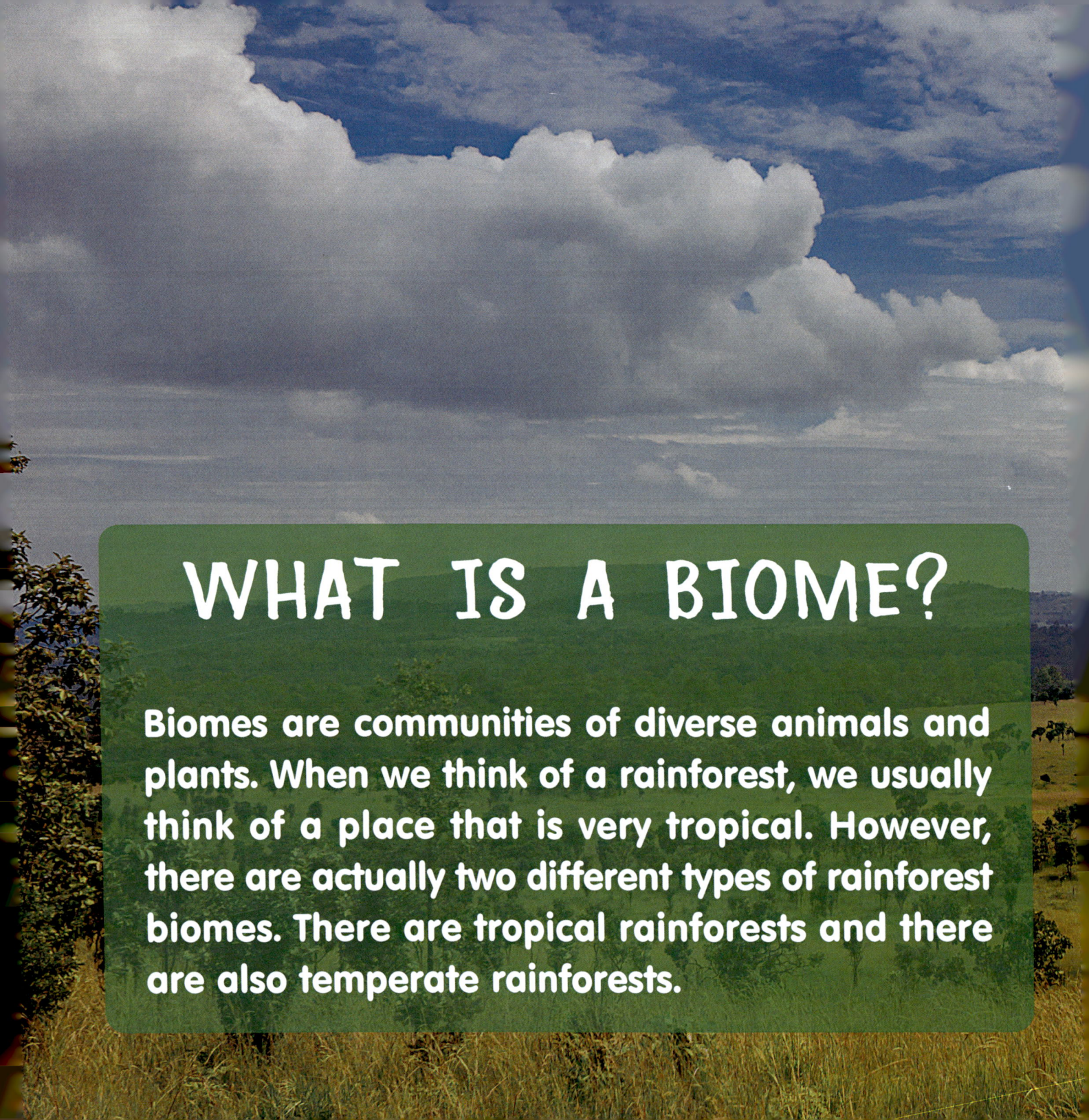

WHAT IS A BIOME?

Biomes are communities of diverse animals and plants. When we think of a rainforest, we usually think of a place that is very tropical. However, there are actually two different types of rainforest biomes. There are tropical rainforests and there are also temperate rainforests.

WHERE ARE TROPICAL RAINFORESTS FOUND?

Tropical rainforests are generally located between the 30-degree north latitude and the 30-degree south latitude. They cover about 7% of the world's landmass surface. Tropical rainforests are found in:

- Central America as well as South America
- The western region of Africa
- The eastern region of Madagascar

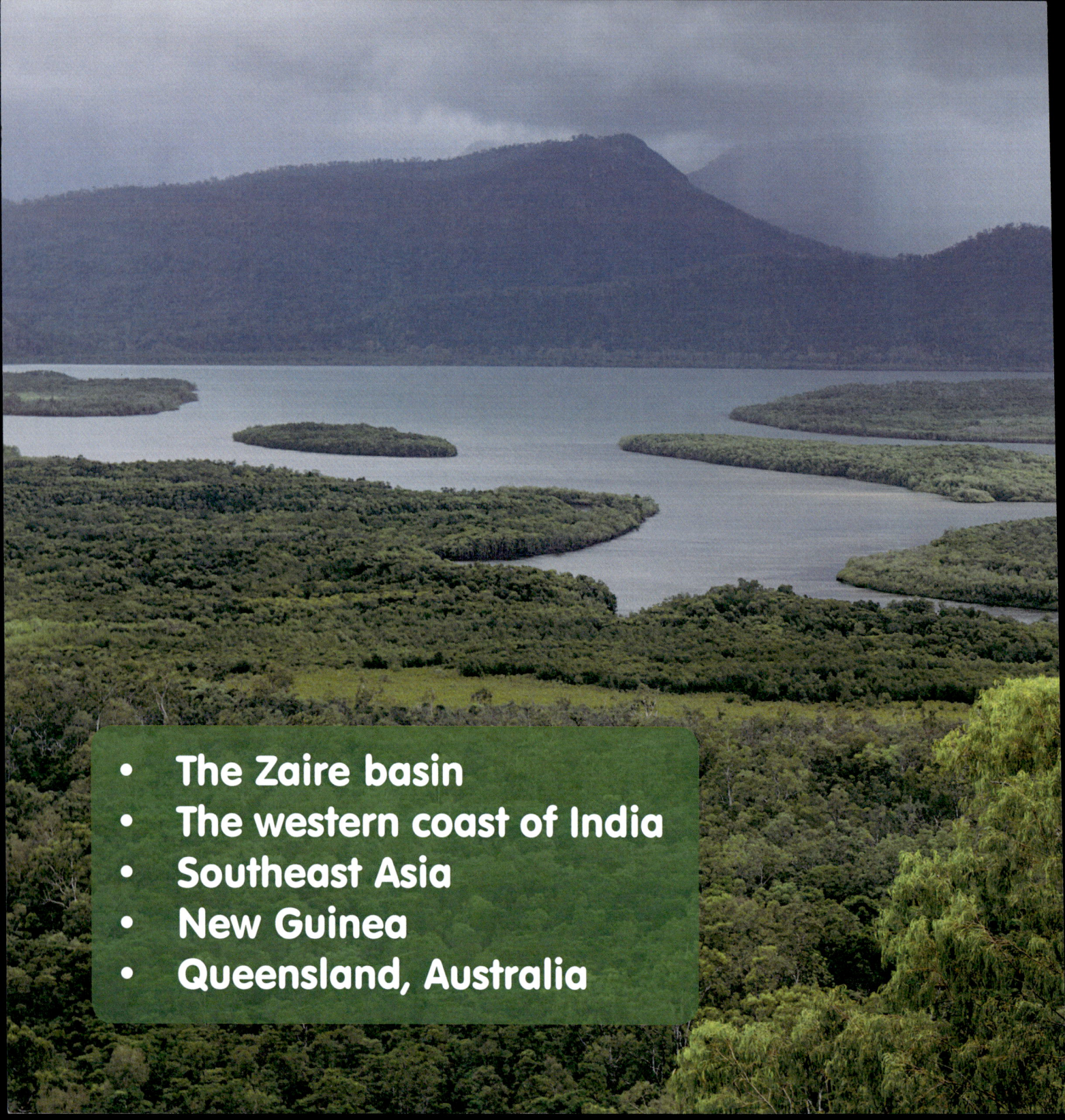

- **The Zaire basin**
- **The western coast of India**
- **Southeast Asia**
- **New Guinea**
- **Queensland, Australia**

QUEENSLAND, AUSTRALIA

WHERE ARE TEMPERATE RAINFORESTS FOUND?

Temperate rainforests are located along the coastlines of regions that have temperate climates. The largest of the temperate rainforests on Earth are found in these locations:

- The Pacific coastline of North America
- The coastline of Chile
- The United Kingdom

- Japan
- New Zealand
- Southern Australia

Waterfall in Tasmania Rainforest, Australia

WHY ARE RAINFORESTS IMPORTANT TO EARTH'S WEATHER?

Rainforests are critically important to the patterns of weather on Earth. Large amounts of rain fall there. The water then evaporates from the surfaces of the trees and later falls in other areas of the Earth as precipitation.

WHAT IS THE TEMPERATURE IN A TROPICAL RAINFOREST?

Tropical rainforests have a tropical climate, which means they are very warm and humid throughout the entire year. The temperature doesn't vary much when the sun goes down unlike other places where after dark it gets much cooler.

The average temperature is about 80 degrees Fahrenheit. It's close to 80% humidity all year round. The yearly rainfall is an enormous amount. It can be as little as 80 inches a year to as much as 400 inches annually. When it rains, sometimes it is a torrential rain. That simply means that it pours down very hard, as much as 2 inches in one hour.

WHAT IS THE TEMPERATURE IN A TEMPERATE RAINFOREST?

Temperate rainforests are certainly wet, but they don't have as much rain annually as tropical rainforests do. The rainfall is generally between 60 inches to 200 inches annually. Coastal fog is dense in these rainforests so the trees and plants get moisture from the fog as well, about 10 inches of precipitation yearly.

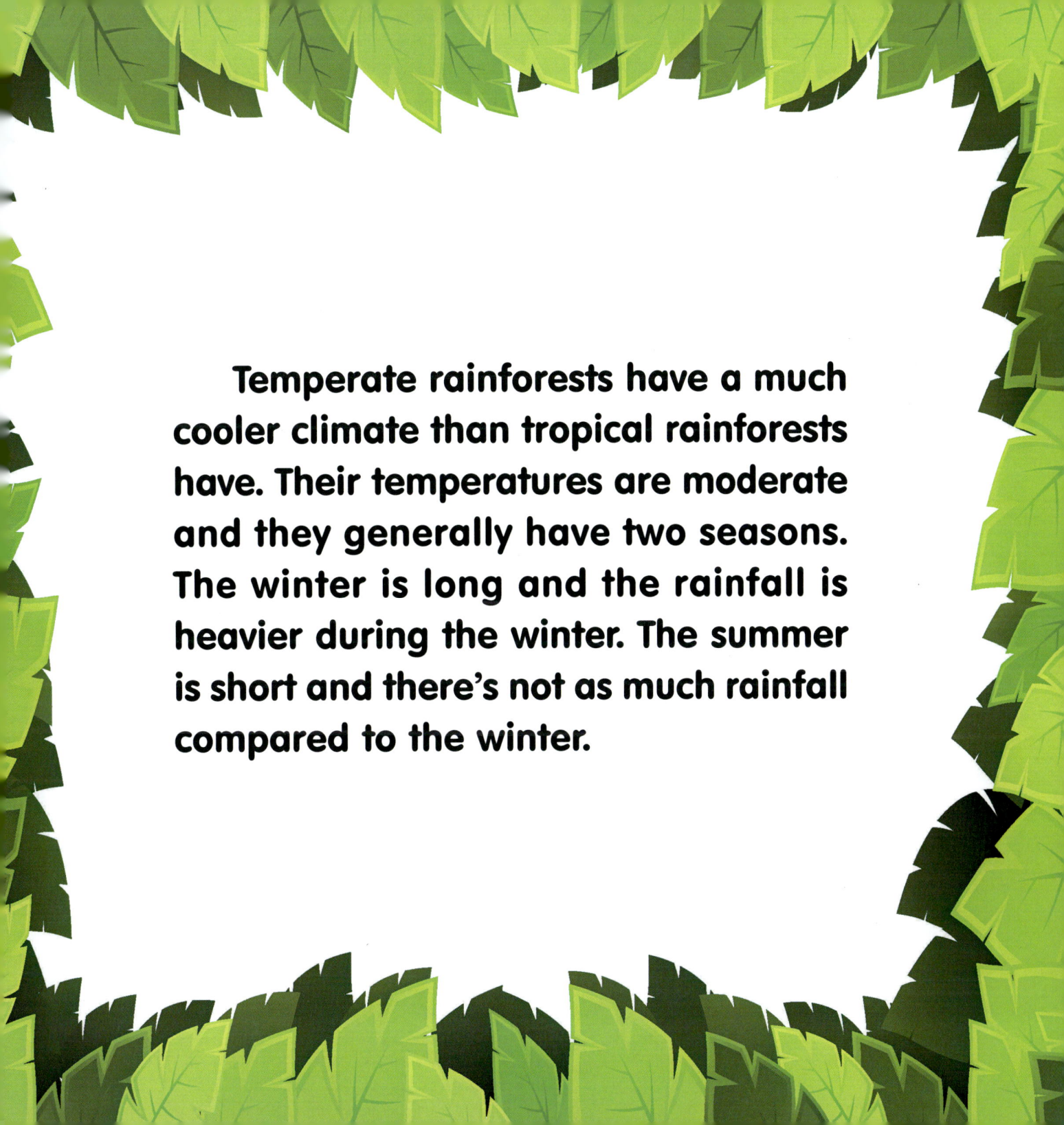

Temperate rainforests have a much cooler climate than tropical rainforests have. Their temperatures are moderate and they generally have two seasons. The winter is long and the rainfall is heavier during the winter. The summer is short and there's not as much rainfall compared to the winter.

WHAT TYPES OF PLANTS GROW IN THE RAINFOREST?

Epiphytes are common in both types of rainforests. These interesting plants grow on the surface of other plants, such as their branches and their trunks. They do this to get sunlight and water. In tropical rainforests, there are many different types of epiphytes. One common type is the bromeliad. Pineapples are examples of bromeliads.

EPIPHYTE ON A TREE

TREE WITH DENSE MOSSES

There are also over 20,000 types of orchids thriving in tropical rainforests. In temperate rainforests, the most common epiphytes are ferns and dense mosses.

Epiphytes aren't parasites. They don't harm their host trees or plants by growing on them. However, they do take water and sunlight that the host plant might need.

WHAT TYPES OF TREES GROW IN THE RAINFOREST?

There are hundreds of different species of trees living in tropical rainforests. They are typically broadleaf types of trees that live from 50 to 100 years. Most of the trees growing in tropical rainforests have a very different type of bark than the bark you would see in another type of forest.

Their trees have very thin bark that's also smooth. They don't need thicker bark because generally the purpose of thicker bark is to keep moisture in. Since it's so wet in the rainforest they don't need this extra insulation.

The reason the bark is smooth is so epiphytes can't easily attach themselves. Because the soil is so wet, trees usually have large ridges that branch out near their bases for extra support. They generally have roots that are fairly shallow, but the trees get tall so they need this support to maintain stability.

These trees sometimes have prop roots to help support them as well. Many rainforest plants and trees have unusual leaf shapes. These shapes have evolved to help precipitation drip off the plant quickly so that bacteria or forms of fungus don't grow on the surfaces of its leaves.

GIANT SEQUOIA TREES

The types of trees that grow in temperate rainforests are very different than the tropical rainforest trees. There are about 20 different species and they are almost all coniferous types, which means they have needles and have cones. Some of these trees, such as the Giant Sequoia, can live for over 1,000 years!

THE ZONES OF A TROPICAL RAINFOREST

Tropical rainforests are so densely packed with trees that scientists divide them into four different zones, starting from top to bottom:

- **The Emergent Layer**—This is the top layer that contains gigantic trees that are much taller than the others

- The Canopy—This layer has trees that are up to 150 feet tall but as short as 60 feet tall. Their branches link to form a canopy like a gigantic umbrella over the forest floor. In addition to the trees, there are very thick vines. Some of these vines, which are known as lianas, have trunks that are as wide as a person's waist. There are over 2,500 species of woody vines in the canopy. These vines need sunlight too, so they climb up the trees as they move upwards toward the sunlight.

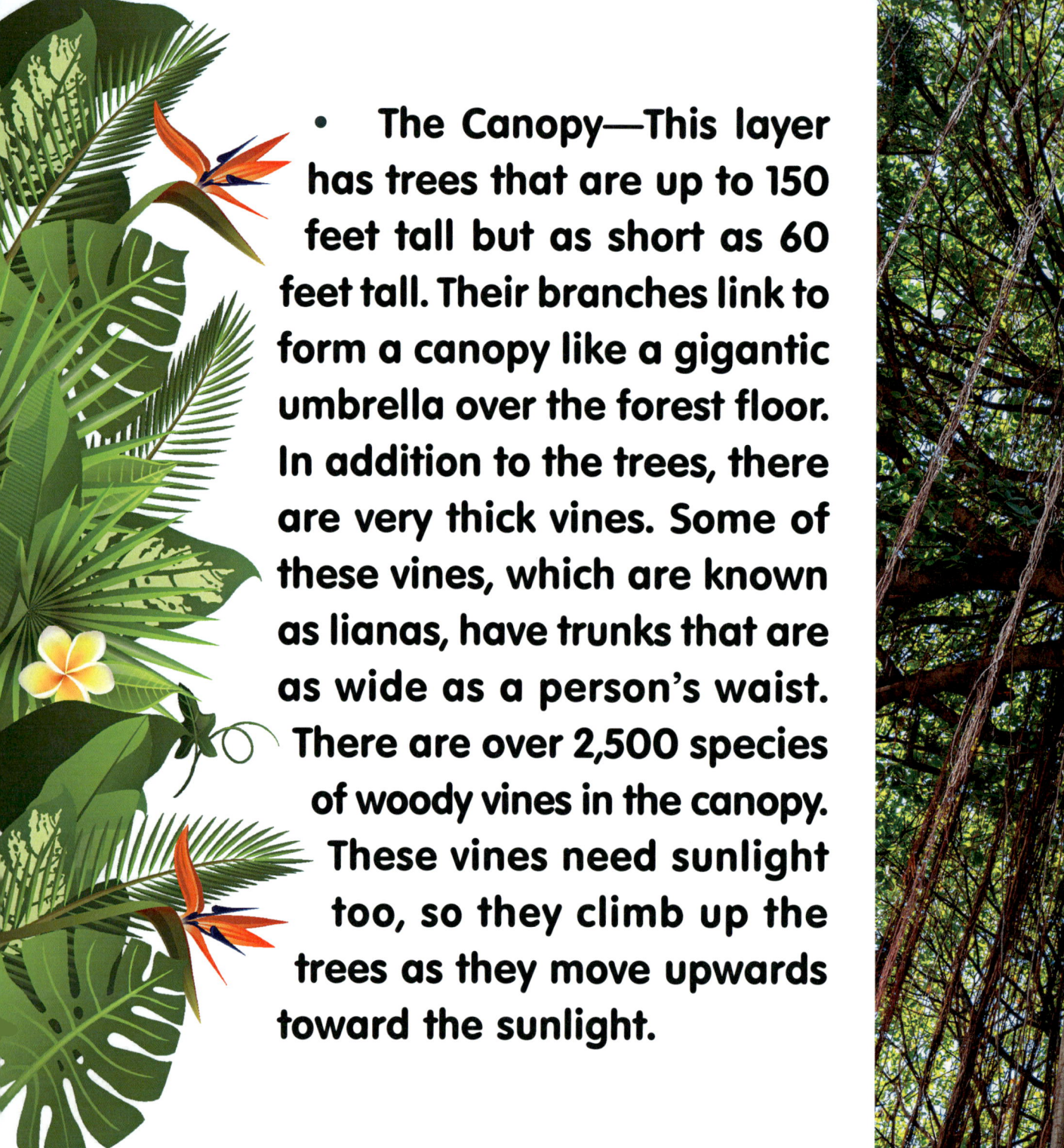

VINE AND LIANAS AROUND A GIANT OLD TREE

- **The Understory**—This is the layer that is dark because the canopy is preventing light from getting through.

- **The Forest Floor**—This is the ground under all the dense trees. Decomposing plant matter is here and there are insects of all types.

Temperate rainforests have these layers except for the emergent layer. The tallest trees in temperate rainforests grow to a height of about 300 feet.

MUSHROOM ON FOREST FLOOR

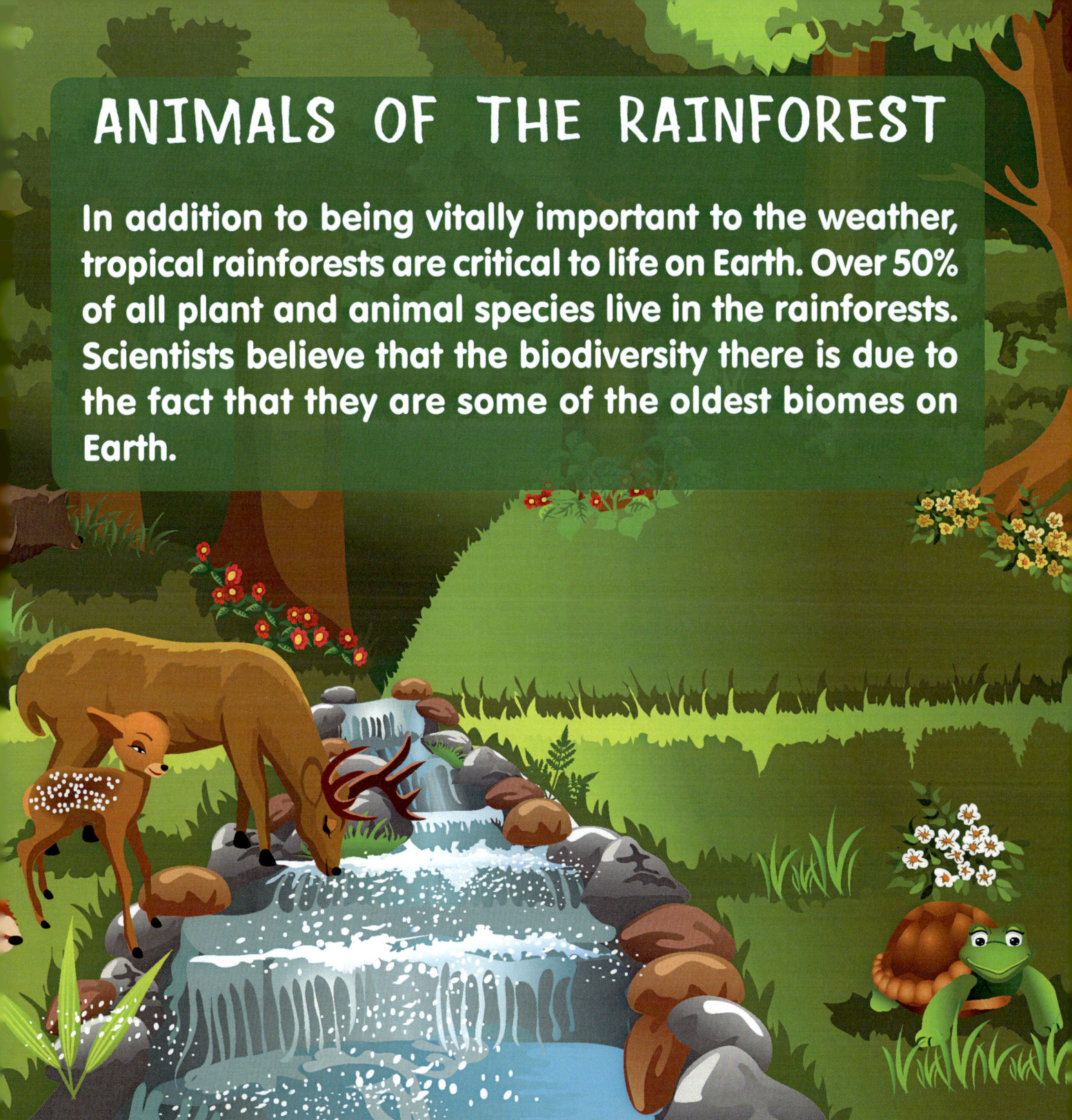

ANIMALS OF THE RAINFOREST

In addition to being vitally important to the weather, tropical rainforests are critical to life on Earth. Over 50% of all plant and animal species live in the rainforests. Scientists believe that the biodiversity there is due to the fact that they are some of the oldest biomes on Earth.

For example, there are some tropical rainforests located in the southeastern region of Asia that have been there for about 100 million years. In other words, those rainforests were around when dinosaurs were still alive.

DINOSAURS IN THE FOREST

MOTHER MONKEY SITTING WITH BABY HANGING UPSIDE DOWN

Rainforest animals have adapted to survive in the climate and conditions of their habitat. Many of these animals have adapted to living most of their lives in the tree canopy. One of the examples of interesting adaptations is the prehensile tail that monkeys in the South American rainforest have. This type of tail allows the monkeys to hang onto the tree with just their tails.

There's such an abundance of food in the tropical rainforest canopy that some animals never venture down onto the floor of the forest. Birds of all types with bright colors and loud voices can be seen in the rainforest. They eat fruits and seeds. When they eliminate, their droppings fall to the floor and grow into new seedlings. Parrots live in the tropical rainforest, but they are not the only types of birds. Over 25% of all bird species live there and many types of birds spend the winter months in the rainforest.

BUTTERFLY SITTING ON THE HAND OF A WOMAN

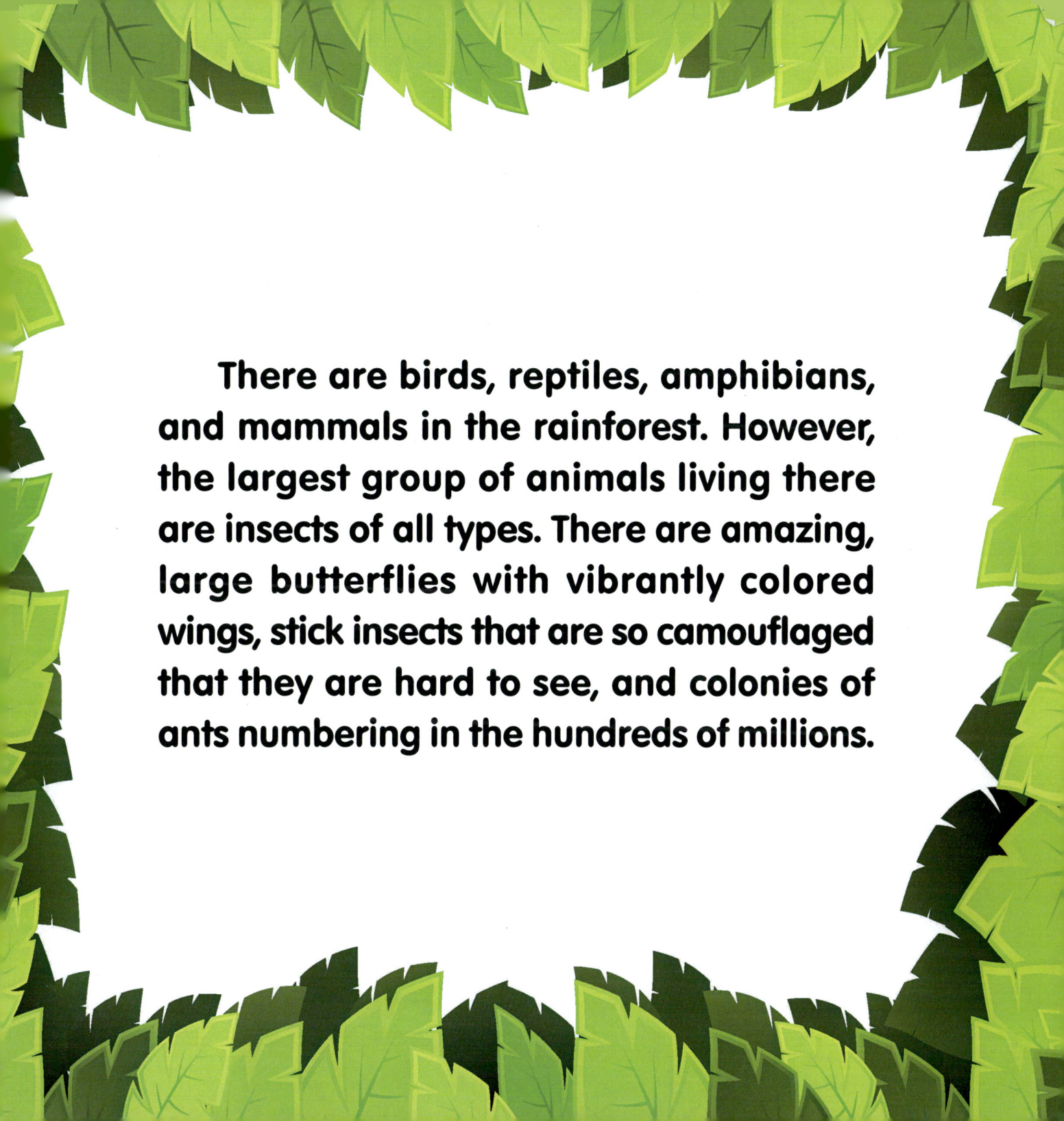

There are birds, reptiles, amphibians, and mammals in the rainforest. However, the largest group of animals living there are insects of all types. There are amazing, large butterflies with vibrantly colored wings, stick insects that are so camouflaged that they are hard to see, and colonies of ants numbering in the hundreds of millions.

In the temperate rainforests, most animals live on the floor of the forest. They live there since the canopy protects them from wind and rain. Many of the birds in the temperate rainforest, as well as the small mammals like chipmunks and squirrels, eat the seeds that fall onto the ground. Many of the insects that live in temperate rainforests survive inside the bark of trees or in plant matter that is decomposing on the forest floor.

SQUIRREL SITS ON A TREE BRANCH ON THE FOREST FLOOR

DEER

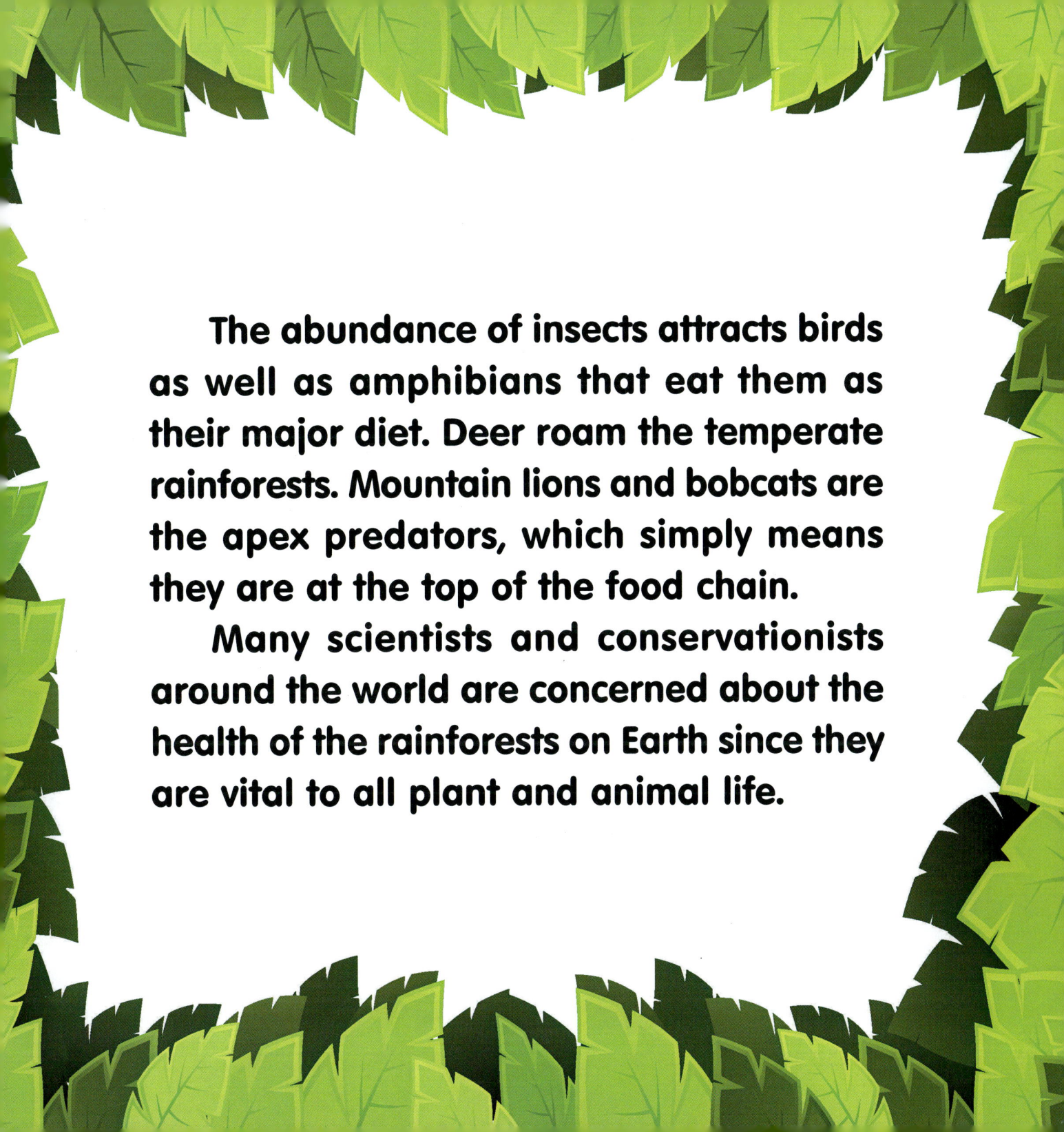

The abundance of insects attracts birds as well as amphibians that eat them as their major diet. Deer roam the temperate rainforests. Mountain lions and bobcats are the apex predators, which simply means they are at the top of the food chain.

Many scientists and conservationists around the world are concerned about the health of the rainforests on Earth since they are vital to all plant and animal life.

SUMMARY

Tropical and temperate rainforests are critical to life on Earth. Although they only cover about 7% of the world's surface, tropical rainforests are home to over 50% of all Earth's animal and plant species. Temperate rainforests contain the oldest trees on the planet. Some of the coniferous trees in temperate rainforests live for over 1,000 years.

Awesome! Now that you've learned about rainforests, you may want to read about one of the world's largest rainforests in the Baby Professor book What Do You Know about the Amazon? Nature for Kids.

Made in United States
North Haven, CT
23 February 2024